My Prayer Buddy Devotional

for a **sisterhood** of **prayer partners**

Janet Holm McHenry

LIVING
INK
BOOKS
Writing Worth Reading™

D1219716

My Prayer Buddy Devotional
Copyright © 2005 by Janet Holm McHenry

Published by Living Ink Books, an imprint of AMG Publishers
6815 Shallowford Rd.
Chattanooga, Tennessee 37421

All rights reserved. Except for brief quotations in printed reviews,
no part of this publication may be reproduced, stored in a retrieval
system or transmitted in any form or by any means (printed, written,
photocopied, visual electronic, audio, or otherwise) without the prior
permission of the publisher.

Unless otherwise indicated, all Scripture quotations are taken from
the HOLY BIBLE, NEW INTERNATIONAL VERSION®. NIV®.
Copyright ©1973, 1978, 1984 by International Bible Society. Used by
permission of Zondervan Publishing House. All rights reserved.

ISBN 0-89957-066-6

First printing—July 2005

Cover designed by Phillip Rodgers, Chattanooga, Tennessee
Interior design and typesetting by Reider Publishing Services,
    West Hollywood, California
Edited and Proofread by Christy Phillippe, Dan Penwell,
    Donna Goodrich, and Rick Steele

Printed in the United States of America
10 09 08 07 06 05 –B– 6 5 4 3 2 1

To my friends in prayer of the Advanced Writers
and Speakers Association, for whom this book is written.
To God be the glory.

JANET HOLM MCHENRY is a speaker and the author of nineteen books, including the following additional books on prayer:

- PrayerWalk: Becoming a Woman of Prayer, Strength, and Discipline
- Daily PrayerWalk: Meditations for a Deeper Prayer Life
- Prayer Changes Teens: How to Parent from Your Knees
- PrayerStreaming: Staying in Touch with God All Day Long

She is the prayer coordinator for the Advanced Writers and Speakers Association and for her church, First Baptist Church of Reno. She speaks widely on prayer, leads a "Moms in Touch" group that prays for teenagers, and organized a prayerwalking ministry in her town in the Sierra Valley in northern California, where she and her husband Craig are raising the last of their four children. You may contact her through her web site, www.dailyprayerwalking.com.

ABOUT AWSA

The Advanced Writers and Speakers Association was founded in 2001 by Linda Evans Shepherd to provide fellowship, prayer support, and encouragement to Christian women who write books and speak. For more information about AWSA, see www.awsawomen.com.

Contents

Introduction

Dear Praying Friend,

So, you've got a prayer partner! How exciting! Whether this is something new for you or something you've done for quite some time, I'm sure you're already realizing you're developing a relationship that is blessing your life beyond measure. You are learning what it means to double your joy and divide your grief.

I've had many partners in prayer over the years—women who have seen me through seasons of sadness and over seemingly insurmountable mountains. We have rejoiced together when babies were born, and we've rejoiced many years later when those "babies" marched across the commencement stage. Frankly, I don't know what I would do without these friends in prayer.

Because we all lead busy lives, the greatest challenge may be to remember to pray. *My Prayer Buddy Devotional* has been designed to encourage you to pray in a different way each week of the year—for strength, for wisdom, for favor, and so on. While your partner will undoubtedly want you to intercede for her and her family's specific requests, *My Prayer Buddy Devotional* will help you to intentionally pray for her deepest spiritual needs. By the end of the year, I feel certain you both will find that you are drawing closer to the Lord and to each other than ever before.

So . . . set aside a special time each day to pray together . . . and then watch what God will begin to do in your lives!

Blessings,
Janet

For Sharpening

SCRIPTURE FOCUS

"As iron sharpens iron, so one man sharpens another."

—PROV. 27:17

God has gifted one of my prayer-walking partners, Pam, with amazing insight. This transfer of his wisdom to her, I believe, has come from her years of study in God's Word. Because of our friendship, I am blessed and sharpened in my own prayer life.

Just this week, I was pretty distressed about several of my kids' problems. Rebekah had gotten my car towed. Justin had lost his wallet with his rent money. Joshua had hurt his knee in a silly motorbike accident on the ranch. They had finally all gone with my husband for a few days of backpacking, so I was home stewing about "what next?"

And then Pam called and reminded me firmly, "Janet, what does God's Word say?"

"Oh, I don't know . . ." I started to whine.

"But you do," she said. "Psalm 32:7 says, 'You are my hiding place; you will protect me from trouble and surround me with songs of deliverance.'"

She was right. As prayer partners, we can remind each other of the promises in God's Word when our feelings overwhelm us and cloud our thinking. As you pray for your friend this week, ask God to use his Word to sharpen her with his promises.

PRAYER FOCUS

"Lord, let your Word sharpen my friend this week."

FRIEND FOCUS

"When my prayer buddy prays for me, I can hear the God-given authority in her voice, even though it's via e-mail."

—EVA MARIE EVERSON

YOUR FOCUS

1. _____

2. _____

3. _____

For Support

SCRIPTURE FOCUS

"Two are better than one, because they have a good return
for their work:
If one falls down, his friend can help him up."

—ECCLES. 4:9, 10

After teaching high school English my first year, I found myself assigned to fourth and fifth graders in my second year. To make matters more complicated, I was pregnant, morning sickness was making me weak, and my portable classroom didn't arrive until two days before school started. Despite these problems, the most confusing predicament, it seemed, was what to put on my bulletin boards—so I called my mom, an artist and a retired teacher. I knew she could get me ready for my first day of school.

In those few days, Mom and I put our heads together, got my room in shape, and constructed all sorts of beautiful bulletin boards all over the room. I was ready . . . at least for Day One!

In the same way, we can be an encouragement to each other when we're struggling in prayer. When I'm so stressed, discouraged, or depressed that I don't even know what to say to the Lord, I can call out to my prayer partner—"Help!"—and she will lovingly come alongside me to pray with me and for me.

Have you heard from your prayer buddy recently? Maybe she needs a prayer lift!

PRAYER FOCUS

"Lord, please help me to encourage my prayer friend this week."

FRIEND FOCUS

"I am thankful for my prayer buddy, who has walked me through a time of testing."

—SHERRIE ELDRIDGE

YOUR FOCUS

1 _____

2 _____

3 _____

For Companionship

SCRIPTURE FOCUS

"If two lie down together, they will keep warm. But how can one keep warm alone?"

—ECCLES. 4:11

Writing can be a lonely life. You sit in your little office, facing a blank screen. No one reminds you that it's break time or asks if you'd like a cup of tea. No one sympathizes when your computer has suddenly become Enemy Number One and refuses to cooperate with even the simplest request.

I recently shared my frustrations with a friend about a current writing project. Finally, I blurted out, "Oh, maybe the Lord will come, and I won't have to finish this book!"

"Janet," she said calmly, "you know that won't happen."

"It won't?" I said, a little stunned by her conviction. I mean, who really knows such things?

"Because he wants you to write this book. Now let me pray you through this time of frustration."

Often cold discouragement creeps into our lives without our even knowing that its presence has begun to chill our relationship with the Lord. Sometimes all we need is just the warmth of prayer a close friend can provide. Perhaps you can be the one to provide that sunny support by praying for your friend this week.

PRAYER FOCUS

"Lord, fill my prayer friend with the warmth of your love this week."

FRIEND FOCUS

"My prayer buddy is an approachable, authentic person who is consistently interested in and praying for my ministry to parents, as well as my personal life."

—BRENDA NIXON

YOUR FOCUS

1 _____

2 _____

3 _____

For Strength

SCRIPTURE FOCUS

"Though one may be overpowered, two can defend themselves.
A cord of three strands is not quickly broken."

—ECCLES. 4:12

I've had a few crazy experiences while prayerwalking.
I've heard bears rumbling in trash bins. I've seen fresh
mountain-lion tracks crossing the street just two houses away
from mine. And I've been chased by a wacky raccoon and
sprayed by a skunk.

The wildest time, though, was when I thought I saw a
drug deal going down one dark, early morning, and then hid
when one of the parties began following me. These incidents
are why I highly recommend a partner when you're prayerwalking. Two are not as easy a target as one person walking
alone.

That's also true in the spiritual realm when you're teamed up in prayer. When you're doing battle in prayer, the enemy can sling all kinds of weapons at you—discouragement, deception, doubt, depression, and despair. During those times of spiritual battle, I need the agreement of my prayer partner. The resulting three-stranded cord—the Lord and the two of us—keeps me praying even more strongly. Get in touch with your prayer buddy this week. Perhaps she needs your agreement in prayer about something important in her life.

PRAYER FOCUS

"Lord, be our third strand so we may stand strong in prayer when danger threatens us."

FRIEND FOCUS

"When our friend was life-flighted for major injuries, I went straight to the Advanced Writers and Speakers Association (AWSA) team for concerted prayer. I have no doubt that his survival is due to these faithful prayer warriors."

—DAYLE SHOCKLEY

YOUR FOCUS

1 _____

2 _____

3 _____

For Agreement

SCRIPTURE FOCUS

"My intercessor is my friend as my eyes pour out tears to
God; on behalf of a man he pleads with God as a man pleads
for his friend."

—JOB 16:20, 21

This fall my daughter Bethany had what I thought were
the First-Day-of-Junior-High-School jitters. Her tummy
hurt so much that she begged to stay home from school.
Although I figured the aches were in her imagination, it
turned out they were actually in her appendix.

With one quick phone call, I asked June to pray. In the
next six hours, I led Bethany through x-rays, CT scans, blood
work and other lab tests, IVs, a respiratory treatment, surgery,
and post-op care.

I hardly had time to think and make decisions, much less
time to pray. But that was okay, because I knew June and our
friends were in prayer on my behalf for Bethany.

A friend who will intercede in prayer is a real encouragement during times of crisis. The Hebrew word for *intercessor* can also be translated as "mediator" and "spokesman." Just as a mediator brings parties together in agreement, an interceding friend pleads for his friend—only before the heavenly Judge. Whether or not the request is ultimately answered as requested, it's still a comfort to know your friend is supporting you with prayer.

Remember to plead on behalf of your prayer friend this week.

PRAYER FOCUS

"Lord, when my friend hurts this week, please meet her deepest needs."

FRIEND FOCUS

"In the toughest time of my marriage and ministry, just when I thought I could not make it another day, the phone rang. My mentor was on the other end, and as she prayed with me aloud, I knew with a newly-found surety that I would make it, too."

—SHARON HOFFMAN

YOUR FOCUS

1 _____

2 _____

3 _____

For Appreciation

SCRIPTURE FOCUS

"I thank my God every time I remember you."

—PHIL. 1:3

There are some friends who always inspire thanks. When my dad died several years ago, I knew I should give the eulogy at his memorial service. It was a logical decision: I'm the oldest of five kids and the writer in the family. But I'm also pretty emotional, so I wasn't sure I could get through the address without breaking down.

The service was held at my parents' church, which was about 200 miles from my hometown. A couple of my friends said they'd try to make the trip, but I knew that would mean a very long day for them on the road. In any case, they had said they'd be praying for me—and that would have been enough.

As folks started to arrive, I remembered something I needed to check in the sanctuary. As I went inside, I found that five very dear friends from my town, including my pastor and his wife, were already seated. Later, when I gave the eulogy—with Dad's own jokes and a few sentimental points—I didn't even need to fight back tears. I knew my friends were praying me through the whole thing.

We can thank God every time we remember our buddies, because we know they're holding us up regularly before the Father in prayer. How would we otherwise get through the day?

Thank the Lord today for your sister in prayer, and pray that others appreciate her as well.

PRAYER FOCUS

"Lord, let many express their thanks this week to my prayer friend for all she is and all she does."

FRIEND FOCUS

"My prayer partner takes time on a regular basis to ask me how she can pray for me, and when I need emergency prayers, I know I can count on her."

—JEANNE GOWEN DENNIS

YOUR FOCUS

1 _____

2 _____

3 _____

For Wisdom

SCRIPTURE FOCUS

"Since the day we heard about you, we have not stopped praying for you and asking God to fill you with the knowledge of his will through all spiritual wisdom and understanding."

—COL. 1:9

Pam and her husband couldn't figure out what God was doing in their lives. Her husband had gotten a job teaching at a Texas university, but their house in North Carolina just would not sell. Even after more than a year of his commuting back on weekends, their house still had not sold.

"I just wish I knew what God was doing!" Pam would e-mail frequently.

I prayed for her daily—that God would bring them back together, and that He would give them discernment to follow His will clearly.

While all the pieces of God's mystery have still not fallen into place, the family is now together in Texas. Even though their East Coast house is still on the market, they know for certain that God is sovereign in their lives, that he has taken care of their deepest needs, and that he has a purpose for their struggles. Knowing the "whys" doesn't seem as important anymore now that they've seen God's faithful provision.

Sometimes steps of faith are hard to take when God's will seems fuzzy. At those particular times of our lives, prayer is crucial. We can pray that our friends will find clear direction through his Word, through prayer, through the counsel of others, and through circumstances.

PRAYER FOCUS

"Lord, please give my prayer partner your wisdom this week as she seeks your will in her life."

FRIEND FOCUS

"When I ask my friend to pray, I know she will go to the Lord and ask him to do what's best, rather than what I think is best."

—MARLENE BAGNULL

YOUR FOCUS

1 _____

2 _____

3 _____

WEEK

8

For Purpose

SCRIPTURE FOCUS

"We constantly pray for you, that our God may count you worthy of his calling, and that by his power he may fulfill every good purpose of yours and every act prompted by your faith."

—2 THESS. 1:11

About seventeen years ago at a women's retreat in the California Sierras, I was sitting on a rock praying when I heard God say, *I want you to write for me*. I was so amazed that I actually stood up. I didn't even know what *write for me* meant, but a short time later at a Christian writers' conference, I quickly learned. I also learned that I was going to need a bunch of prayer buddies so my writing would indeed be for the Lord and not for myself.

Today I sent out another prayer letter to twenty-five or so folks, most of whom have been praying for me all these years. They've now seen me through the writing of nineteen books—and ten times that number in rejections. As I thought tonight about the privilege of the work I do, I realized that I'm really *not* worthy of my calling. However, my friends have been praying that God will "count"—or "make"—me worthy anyway.

Praying that our friend knows God's purpose for her life is so important, as it will help her make the smaller decisions day by day. Having that vision will help her say "yes" to the things of God and "no" to the things that aren't in his will. Pray that she hears God's clear voice and direction for her life.

PRAYER FOCUS

"Father, make your purpose for my friend's life very clear to her, so that she can choose the right daily steps."

FRIEND FOCUS

"A prayer partner keeps me focused on intercession for the world, friends, and family, and she doubles the praise and thanksgiving when God answers."

—JANET CHESTER BLY

YOUR FOCUS

1 _____

2 _____

3 _____

For Camaraderie

SCRIPTURE FOCUS

"Jesus said, 'I no longer call you servants, because a servant does not know his master's business. Instead, I have called you friends, for everything that I learned from my Father I have made known to you.'"

—JOHN 15:15

June and I talk every day on the phone. We share the highs and lows of the previous twenty-four hours—often things we would share with no one else. Also prayerwalking partners, we dump our disappointments on each other as we head out on the highway at five in the morning. After a time of prayer together that clears our heads and hearts, we're ready to intercede for the thousand folks in our mountain town.

Serving and praying together builds intimacy and trust. Jesus became more than just partners with his dozen disciples. This week's verse shows that he called them his friends as well, because of his sharing what the Father had taught him. They were, in effect, each other's confidantes.

The word *confidant* (feminine: *confidante*) comes from a French word that means "confident" or "trustworthy." When we share our needs with each other, we become confident and trustworthy confidantes, the one special person to whom the other can run with a request for prayer.

Perhaps your prayer buddy needs a confidante today. Call her or send an e-mail and ask how you can encourage her and pray for her needs.

PRAYER FOCUS

"Lord, meet my friend's needs for camaraderie—through me and others who will be there for her through thick and thin."

FRIEND FOCUS

"What a joy to finally meet my prayer buddy, to sense her closeness to Christ, and to see the glow on her face!"
—CHARLOTTE ADELSPERGER

YOUR FOCUS

1 _____

2 _____

3 _____

For Deliverance

SCRIPTURE FOCUS

"I will continue to rejoice, for I know that through your prayers and the help given by the Spirit of Jesus Christ, what has happened to me will turn out for my deliverance."

—PHIL. 1:18,19

In April of this year, I found myself facing my greatest fear. I was flat in bed, with back surgery imminent. I had herniated a disc and couldn't walk, stand, or even sit. Even worse, I could not prayerwalk. In the previous several years, it had become my passion to pray for my small community while I walked in the early morning hours. If I couldn't walk, how could my town be covered in prayer?

After a few phone calls, I realized that friends all over the country were praying for me—not only for healing, but also for my ministry of intercession. And guess what? Just as Paul found his ministry expanded within the prison walls, I found that mine grew as well. My church joined in on the ministry, and together we recruited about twenty men and women to prayerwalk—even expanding the prayerwalking area. Because of my "imprisonment" in bed, God's work expanded.

Perhaps your prayer partner feels imprisoned—by illness, circumstances, or a difficult job. Our God is in the business of breaking chains. Remember her in prayer, and just see what God will do!

PRAYER FOCUS

"Lord, deliver my friend from any chains that bind and discourage her."

FRIEND FOCUS

"Just as Aaron and Hur held up Moses' arms so he could do God's work when he was at his most weary, there are people in my life who hold mine up. Their prayers have sustained me so that I could complete the work God has given me to do."

—VICKI CARUANA

YOUR FOCUS

1 _____
2 _____
3 _____

For Faith

SCRIPTURE FOCUS

"Brothers, my heart's desire and prayer to God for the Israelites is that they may be saved."

—ROM. 10:1

When our church split years ago over leadership differences, my son Justin, now twenty-four, was a junior in high school. The resulting struggles affected him greatly, and once he left home he stopped going to church. Soon he seemed to take on the cynicism often prevalent in university settings. Our discussions about the faith were tense, at best.

At a recent retreat, my friend Barbara approached me and asked, "How can I pray for you?" She then interceded for my son—that he would return to the faith of his youth and recommit his life to Christ. She also prayed for me—that I would rest in faith that God would take care of my son.

Within the week I got a phone call from Justin. He was excited to report that he was taking a "great course" on the origins of Christianity—and that the lecturer hired for the class was actually a Christian minister. Over the course of the next couple of months, Justin and I had amazing discussions about the authenticity of the faith—exactly the issue he was debating when he pulled away from the church.

I thank God for my prayer sister who prayed for my son. Why don't you contact your prayer friend today and find out what loved ones of hers need your prayers for salvation?

PRAYER FOCUS

"Father, bring to faith those my friend loves and increase her own faith as well."

FRIEND FOCUS

"My friend suggested one day that we pray the promises, not the problems. We began praising God that he is a God who finishes the work he begins."

—JAN COLEMAN

YOUR FOCUS

1 _____

2 _____

3 _____

For Answers

SCRIPTURE FOCUS

"Jesus said, 'Father, I thank you that you have heard me.'"

—JOHN 11:41

Years ago when I worked for my husband in his law office, we customarily closed letters with this statement: "Thank you for your anticipated cooperation." I didn't realize until recently that this echoes one of Jesus' prayers.

Before Jesus called out to his friend Lazarus, who had been laid dead into a tomb, he thanked his Father for hearing his prayer. Isn't that amazing? Jesus thanked God before the prayer was even answered. I don't know about you, but I'd been in the habit of giving thanks only after the answer was right before my eyes.

This simple principle has changed the way I pray: I've become expectantly thankful along with my requests. As I pray, I thank God for the answers that are ahead and then joyfully wait.

When the brother of a friend of mine was in a coma recently, my friend asked me to pray that God would speak to him through his sleep. I prayed daily that Carl would meet Christ in this way, and one day my friend experienced peace that God had done just that—just days before Carl died. We believe that my friend will have a reunion with her brother in heaven.

As you lift your prayer sister up before the Lord this week, thank him for hearing your requests made on her behalf . . . and then just see what he will do!

PRAYER FOCUS

"Lord, I thank you for meeting the deepest needs of my prayer friend."

FRIEND FOCUS

"I called my prayer sister recently to share exciting break-through news. She said, 'This morning I prayed that everything you touched today would turn to gold!'"

—JILL RIGBY

YOUR FOCUS

1. _____

2. _____

3. _____

For Healing

SCRIPTURE FOCUS

"Therefore confess your sins to each other and pray for each other so that you may be healed. The prayer of a righteous man is powerful and effective."

—JAMES 5:16

When I was struggling recently to lose the weight I had gained from my back injury and surgery, I told a teacher friend at work. She said she'd been struggling, too, and suggested that we encourage and pray for each other, as well as join a weight-loss group together. Before the school year ended, I had met my weight goal. Now, two years later, we still pray for and encourage each other to stay on track—even continuing to exercise together.

Sometimes we need physical healing, and sometimes we have emotional damage that needs healing. That's when a prayer partner can help. She not only can pray for you, but she can also come alongside you to help you take those practical steps that can change your life. Just knowing you have someone praying for you can be that powerful and effective push to spur you on to better health—a stronger body, a restored relationship, a conquered habit, and a deeper trust in God, who also wants wholeness in our lives.

When you are open with your prayer partner, sharing your weaknesses and needs for prayer, it will be easier for her to open up to you. That's when real friendship and prayer partnership develop. When your prayer buddy trusts you with her heartfelt confession, pray for her and encourage her to take steps toward healing.

PRAYER FOCUS

"Father, heal my friend and help us to be open with each other, so that your power may be magnified through our lives."

FRIEND FOCUS

"Most girlfriends will give you a pep talk or a Kleenex when you're down or just in a mood, but my good friend always prays for me. Once when we were both discouraged at a writers' conference, we prayed right in the corridor for one another to keep our focus on an audience of One."

—LESLIE VERNICK

YOUR FOCUS

1 _____

2 _____

3 _____

For Partnership

SCRIPTURE FOCUS

"In all my prayers for all of you, I always pray with joy because of your partnership in the gospel from the first day until now."

—PHIL. 1:4, 5

My friend, Anne, has loved each one of my kids. As our church's youth leader, she has counseled them, prayed with them, baked them cookies, taken them on mission trips, taught them the Bible, corrected them . . . but most importantly, loved them.

She called me tonight. Among other things, she told me she had never realized how funny Josh is—that he and his friend Jonathan were absolutely cracking her up in the car with their jokes on the way to their Mexico mission meeting. "He is just so fun to be with," she said.

The thing is, Anne seeks out my kids—and other parents' kids—even when they're not fun to be with. I totally sense her prayer partnership with me as I do my best to guide my children. Because of this, she is the one I call first when I see joyful answers to prayer in my kids' lives.

Our moms and grandmas said, "Many hands make light work." That's true for the prayer burdens of our hearts, too. When there's deep, long-term prayer work to do, the season seems shorter when you know your friend is praying as well. Check with your prayer buddy and find out how you can make her prayer work lighter this week.

PRAYER FOCUS

"Lord, may my prayers make my friend's work lighter as she spreads your Word."

FRIEND FOCUS

"There is a sisterhood among the author members of AWSA that creates a bond of love, respect, and support resembling a threefold cord that cannot be broken."
—THELMA WELLS

YOUR FOCUS

1 _____

2 _____

3 _____

For Reputation

SCRIPTURE FOCUS

"We always thank God, the Father of our Lord Jesus Christ, when we pray for you, because we have heard of your faith in Christ Jesus and of the love you have for all the saints."

—COL. 1:3, 4

Some of my best friends I've never met. In fact, some of my closest partners in prayer I wouldn't even recognize if I met them face-to-face. How is that? E-mail, of course. I'm involved with several large e-mail prayer circles—of writers and of parents of teenagers. Almost daily we pour out our hearts to one another, and then we take each other's needs to the Lord.

This isn't a completely new phenomena. When Paul wrote the letter to the Colossians, telling them that he always thanked God for them, he had not met them either. It was his friend and associate, Ephaphras, who had taken the gospel message to Colossae after hearing Paul preach in Ephesus and embracing the faith.

Through our prayers back and forth, we learn of each other's faith walks. Sometimes it's a little scary sharing deep concerns. Others could judge us, or our reputations could take a bruising. But every family struggles in some way, and knowing that you have a friend who's dedicated to you can make all the difference when life gets challenging. Remember to pray for your friend this week—that her reputation will be spotless and that she will confide in you with her deepest struggles.

PRAYER FOCUS

"Father, protect my friend when others seek to damage her reputation."

FRIEND FOCUS

"Confidentiality and candor are a blessed mix in the partnership that establishes a deep sense of sisterhood and an indescribable comfort, knowing that another is helping to bear your burdens or joining in your joy."
—PAMELA CHRISTIAN

YOUR FOCUS

1 _____

2 _____

3 _____

For Service

SCRIPTURE FOCUS

"Finally, brothers, pray for us that the message of the Lord may spread rapidly and be honored, just as it was with you."

—2 THESS. 3:1

I received an e-mail tonight from "Becca," whom I've never met. She's eighteen, and it's her heart's desire to someday be a speaker to young girls. She wrote to me because she knew I was a communicator, and she wanted some advice about her future education. "Where should I go to college if I want to do what you're doing?" she wrote.

Each of us has the opportunity to serve Christ in some significant way. One friend collects eyeglasses to take to South America. Another solicits hotel samples to give to women in prison. Yet another raises funds and awareness about refugee children in Africa. When a friend takes these giant steps of faith and faces the risks that accompany them, she will need and appreciate my prayers of support.

Paul relied upon the churches to intercede for him as he took the gospel message from city to city, and he expected that their prayers would have results. Part of our partnership with our prayer friend is an investment of spiritual energy as we commit to praying for her as she ministers—as a Sunday school teacher, a member of the praise band, or a helper in a soup kitchen. However she serves, she will be open to criticism and attack from the enemy—so those prayers of protection and anointing are especially needed. Remember to hold her up in prayer this week!

PRAYER FOCUS

"Lord God, protect my friend this week as she serves you— and may you be honored through everything she does."

FRIEND FOCUS

"Although my prayer partner and I both have busy schedules, we always take a moment to e-mail each other a quick prayer request or praise report."

—SUSAN TITUS OSBORN

YOUR FOCUS

1 _____

2 _____

3 _____

17

For Favor

SCRIPTURE FOCUS

"On him we have set our hope that he will continue to deliver us, as you help us by your prayers. Then many will give thanks on our behalf for the gracious favor granted us in answer to the prayers of many."

—2 COR. 1:10, 11

When my daughter Rebekah went on a mission to Turkey several years ago with a half dozen others, I knew that she'd be all right, even though the country is more than 99 percent Muslim, and even though they'd have to share their faith surreptitiously. She and the other college students had taken funds to give to those in need following a major earthquake, but they mostly hoped to tell others about Christ.

I still didn't worry when I learned that several Christians were found dead alongside Turkish roads . . . when I learned

Rebekah and her friends were being followed . . . and even when I found out that policemen had searched their rooms and threatened them. I knew that dozens, perhaps hundreds, were partnering in prayer as those young people were visiting some of the same cities that Paul and his partners did—the same places where he had "despaired even of life" because of physical persecution (1 Cor. 1:8).

Just as Paul could boldly step out and do what God had called him to do—because of others' prayers for him—your prayer partner can also confidently follow the Spirit's leading in her life as you remember her in prayer. I'm sure she'd also appreciate a little note or call that lets her know she's in your thoughts and prayers.

PRAYER FOCUS

"Father, pour your favor on my friend this week as she determines to set her hope on you."

FRIEND FOCUS

"I never cease to be amazed at the explosively powerful victories I've experienced when my prayer-warrior buddies step into battle on my behalf—it's like C-4 sprinkled with nitro!"

—RHONDA RHEA

YOUR FOCUS

1 _____

2 _____

3 _____

For Fellowship

SCRIPTURE FOCUS

"Pray for us. We are sure that we have a clear conscience and desire to live honorably in every way. I particularly urge you to pray so that I may be restored to you soon."

—HEB. 13:18, 19

My friend Pam can tell me anything—that I have bad breath, that I snore, even that my behavior needs correcting—and I would receive those words with appreciation. There is such honesty, trust, and acceptance between us that I know whatever she tells me is said because of her love for me and her deep desire to see me grow in Christ.

We've prayed each other through work junk, church junk, and kid junk. When she moved across the country, I cried for days. When I had needed prayer, she'd say, "I'll be right there." Now who would come when I was facing the "junk" of my life?

E-mail friends and phone friends across the miles are great, but sometimes we just long for a real hug along with our friend's prayer. If you can't have face-to-face, hand-holding time with your friend, pray that God will provide fellowship for her so that those arms of Christ can wrap up your friend in love. And if you are privileged with her company, give thanks that God has gifted you with her presence.

A week ago I was writing an e-mail note to Pam when I heard my front door open and these words: "Hello! Now who else would walk in your front door without knocking?" It was Pam, and I got a good, long hug!

PRAYER FOCUS

"Father, please provide sweet fellowship for my prayer sister this week and allow us to get together soon."

FRIEND FOCUS

"The most intimate friendships in my life have been forged in prayer partnerships, where two hearts come together to petition the Lord for guidance or help. There's no way to maintain a surface friendship when you've truly prayed together."

—SHIRLEY BRINKERHOFF

YOUR FOCUS

1 _____

2 _____

3 _____

For Grace

SCRIPTURE FOCUS

"And in their prayers for you their hearts will go out to you, because of the surpassing grace God has given you."

—2 COR. 9:14

When I was lying flat in bed before and after my back surgery a few years ago, a dear friend sent me a lovely care package, complete with two pairs of pajamas, slippers, a candle, books on tape, and more. I was stunned. Her giving was over the top. Also more than generous, another friend told me she had stayed up all night to pray for me. "I knew your pain was more than you could bear," she said.

That's just what God's surpassing grace is like—over the top—to have given us the gift of the life of his Son, Jesus Christ, so that we might have life. The word translated *surpassing* or *exceeding* means "to throw over or beyond." His grace is so great, it's like a home run hit out of sight into the San Francisco Bay—it's beyond what we could ever imagine.

The friends God brings into our lives are a reminder of his goodness toward us. When we sacrifice our time or give generously for the sake of one of his children, I think he must delight in these graces of encouragement, practical help, and prayers. Remember your buddy this week, with a prayer of thanks for the graces she has extended to you and others, and for her passing along the indescribable gift.

PRAYER FOCUS

"Lord, grace my friend with your love this week, just as you have graced me."

FRIEND FOCUS

"My friend's most poignant prayer for me was during my son's trial for first-degree murder. God did not answer our prayer in the way we wanted, but he did answer our prayer, and my friend was there to catch my tears."

—CAROL KENT

YOUR FOCUS

1 _____

2 _____

3 _____

For Neighbors

SCRIPTURE FOCUS

"If my people, who are called by my name, will humble themselves and pray and seek my face and turn from their wicked ways, then will I hear from heaven and will forgive their sin and will heal their land. Now my eyes will be open and my ears attentive to the prayers offered in this place."

—2 CHRON. 7:14, 15

My prayerwalking territory is my little town in the Sierra Nevada: Loyalton, population 1,192. Each weekday morning at five, I layer up, grab my walking poles, and pray up and down Main Street. I pray for the business owners by name, for those driving by, for the neighbors whose homes I pass, and for any spiritual issues God may press upon my heart relating to my town.

One way to pray for our friend is to pray for her neighbors—that they will come into a personal relationship with God and delight him with their lives. We can also ask our friend if she has any prayer requests that relate to her community. Perhaps there has been a recent natural disaster in her area. Maybe she is burdened by symptoms indicative of indifference—blight, graffiti, or crime. Perhaps she sees needy children or broken families. We can lighten our friends' burdens by praying for those things that concern her.

When you walk or drive through your town, remember to pray for your friend and her neighborhood and community.

PRAYER FOCUS

"Sovereign Lord, cause those in my friend's neighborhood and town to humble themselves, confess their sins, and live their lives for your glory."

FRIEND FOCUS

"Having prayer partners forces me to 'keep the curtains open' in my life so that the light of Christ can continually show me his truth, his wisdom, his love, and his faithfulness."

—REBECCA BARLOW JORDAN

YOUR FOCUS

1 _____

2 _____

3 _____

For Love

SCRIPTURE FOCUS

"May the Lord make your love increase and overflow for each other and for everyone else, just as ours does for you."

—1 THESS. 3:12

I should have been a counselor, because I love giving all of my friends advice. Sometimes, though, that's not what they need. One time a dear friend told me, "Janet, if I'd wanted advice, I would have asked for it. Instead, I just needed to know I was loved."

I have appreciated my friend's honest words and have learned from them. Instead of automatically spilling my "pearls of wisdom," I'll sympathize and tell a friend I love her. Okay . . . I'll admit it: If I'm really itching, I might ask her if she wants advice. However, along with my intercessions for any specific needs, I also pray that our friendship will grow in love—and that God can use me to demonstrate his compassion.

Often when we receive prayer requests from our friends, we may have the tendency to share advice, when the better course is to go directly to the Problem Solver. He knows exactly what our friend needs. Praying faithfully—through the ups and downs, the darkness and the lighter days, the questions and answers—is a clear demonstration of love. But it's nice to hear or see via e-mail or a handwritten note, "I love you, friend."

As our love overflows for our friend in prayer, perhaps others, too, will benefit from our boundless gift. Remember to tell your prayer partner that you love her this week.

PRAYER FOCUS

"Father, give my friend an extra dose of your love this week."

FRIEND FOCUS

"When our thirty-nine-year-old daughter was killed on Thanksgiving night, 2001, by a drunk driver, our world crumbled around us. In the days and weeks ahead, my AWSA sisters rallied together to pray for God's mercy to comfort all of us."

—CAROLE LEWIS

YOUR FOCUS

1 _____

2 _____

3 _____

For Needs

SCRIPTURE FOCUS

"Night and day we pray most earnestly that we may see you again and supply what is lacking in your faith."

—1 THESS. 3:10

I had sensed for some time that my seventeen-year-old son had been making bad choices, but I didn't have any concrete evidence other than an often-surly attitude and an unwillingness to go to church or youth group. When I found a cigarette in one of his pants pockets, I knew I was only looking at the tip of an iceberg. My first reaction was a sense of hopelessness. Was God really in control? Why hadn't he answered my prayers? Did he care at all?

I dumped my worries on my friend June. Somehow she had made it through her sons' turbulent time of adolescence years ago. She gently reminded me that "With man this is impossible, but with God all things are possible" (Matt. 19:26).

Eight years later, my husband and I are still waiting for our prodigal's return to the faith, but I know that God will do the impossible, because so many partners in prayer are lifting up his name week after week.

It's humanly normal to question God when the problems of life tear at the fringes of our faith. We need each other to mend those frayed parts of our souls so that we don't feel alone, and so that we can be reminded of God's promises at just the right times. Perhaps your prayer friend needs that encouragement today. Call her or send her a note to remind her of how faithful our Lord is.

PRAYER FOCUS

"Lord, meet my friend's deepest needs this week—answer our prayers with the seemingly impossible."

FRIEND FOCUS

"My prayer sisters are like the lifesaver one throws to a drowning friend on the ocean of stress and personal crisis. My praying sisters hold my head above water by turning my face toward the Savior."

—PAM FARREL

YOUR FOCUS

1 _____

2 _____

3 _____

For Mistakes

SCRIPTURE FOCUS

"Now we pray to God that you will not do anything wrong. Not that people will see that we have stood the test but that you will do what is right even though we may seem to have failed."

—2 COR. 13:7

As a high school teacher, I've learned a lot from my peers. "Have several graded assignments each week." "Never assume your students know how to do something. Always teach them, even if it seems repetitive." "Establish classroom routines." There are dozens of stories behind each piece of advice—and I've heard many from other teachers. I'd rather learn from other teachers' mistakes than from my own!

When I do inevitably make a mistake, I'm grateful that I teach with staff members who willingly pray for each other. At a faculty meeting recently, I let my frustrations spill over.

While many agreed with me, I asked a friend to pray for me about the situation, and it soon became clear that I'd offended one of the teachers. Quickly thereafter, I asked for that person's forgiveness. If I'd not asked for prayer, I might not have known to make amends.

Similarly, our prayer partner will make mistakes and mis-judgments—some of which could create serious problems. As we're building a sense of trust with one another, hopefully we're also confiding in each other more—enough to admit our mistakes and ask for God's grace to help us when we do slip up. Remember your buddy this week!

PRAYER FOCUS

"Lord, may your grace cover any mistakes my friend in prayer may make this week."

FRIEND FOCUS

"The security of knowing true acceptance and love in the midst of asking for prayer about personal struggles is the best gift my prayer partner gives me."

—KATHY COLLARD MILLER

YOUR FOCUS

1 _____

2 _____

3 _____

For Growth

SCRIPTURE FOCUS

"We are glad whenever we are weak but you are strong; and our prayer is for your perfection."

—2 COR. 13:9

I work in an office alone, but I am prayed for and encouraged by dozens of women-who-know-what-my-life-is-like, including Cindy, who came up with that expression. What the casual observer would find odd is that these women could be called my competitors. We are all authors and writers. In practical terms, there are only so many book contracts and speaking engagements in a given year in this country. Someone will speak; someone will not. Someone will be published; someone will not. Some years are busy, and some are not.

Despite these facts of life, we still continue to pray for and encourage one another. We cheer when a publishing committee says, "Yes!" We give each other tips and critiques, all for the purpose of helping one another become better writers or speakers. Why do we do that? Because each of us has a different call, a different God-given plan. God doesn't want me to be Thelma Wells or Patsy Clairmont or even Cindy Secrest McDowell, even if I do know what her life is like! God wants me to be the best Janet possible.

Therefore, we need our friends' prayers—that we will be the best we can be, so that God is glorified through whatever we do. When we pray for our sister's growth in her call to follow Christ and in service to him, she wins and we win, too—because we're both growing closer to the Lord we love.

PRAYER FOCUS

"Father, encourage my friend to grow and follow you more closely in her life."

FRIEND FOCUS

"My prayer partner has helped me to move from having a prayer life to embracing a *praying* life. She not only weaves prayer into her life, but she demonstrates that prayer is the very fabric of life itself."

—LYNN MORRISSEY

YOUR FOCUS

1 _____

2 _____

3 _____

WEEK

25

For Celebration

SCRIPTURE FOCUS

"For this reason, ever since I heard about your faith in the Lord Jesus and your love for all the saints, I have not stopped giving thanks for you, remembering you in my prayers."

—EPH. 1:15, 16

Last week one of my students left me a Valentine and some candy kisses on my desk. Strangely though, Lizz wasn't in my class that day. Later when I saw her, she told me that she and her adopted dad had visited her birth father, who was suffering from heart problems in the hospital. The two visitors had shared the gospel message with the ill man, who then proclaimed Christ as his Savior and Lord. Lizz was beaming, and I told her I'd join with her in her prayers for her birth dad.

I appreciate having friends who remind me of the celebration-worthy blessings in my life—my husband and kids, my good job and ministry, and my home, even with its aging flaws. I'm way too reflective sometimes, and I occasionally need a nudge to remember all of the good things in my life.

Additionally, just having a prayer partner is praiseworthy. Increasingly as life passes, you're probably finding that a close friendship—having a prayer-filled relationship and contact with someone weekly—is a rarity. Life is overflowing with activity, and friendships are often squeezed out. Taking time to touch base, share needs, and praise God for the blessings we have and for one another can often be the best part of our week. And that's worth celebrating!

PRAYER FOCUS

"Father, I give you thanks and praise for blessing me with such a good friend. Please bless her with something to celebrate this week."

FRIEND FOCUS

"My life has been transformed because of the prayers of friends. It's great to have heart companions to share my deepest concerns and greatest joys!"

—TRICIA GOYER

YOUR FOCUS

1 _____

2 _____

3 _____

For Revelation

SCRIPTURE FOCUS

"I keep asking that the God of our Lord Jesus Christ, the glorious Father, may give you the Spirit of wisdom and revelation, so that you may know him better."

—EPH. 1:17

The greatest desire of my life is to know God better. In fact, I think if I could know more about God's nature, so many pieces would fall together in my life's puzzle. I'd worry less because I would be trusting him more. Anger wouldn't be a problem, because I'd know there was a reason behind every frustration or trial in my life. I would be more expectant and find greater joy during my days.

I'm learning to know my glorious Father better by reading about him. I love this God who would open the mouth of a donkey to wake up Balaam (Num. 22). Or sympathize with an overwhelmed Moses and give him seventy helpers

(Num. 11). Or provide one of the dearest blessings ever written: "The LORD bless you and keep you; the LORD make his face shine upon you and be gracious to you; the LORD turn his face toward you and give you peace" (Num. 6:24–26). Those are just a few glimpses into God's character—from the book in the Bible many choose to ignore.

As you pray that your prayer partner knows God better, she will find greater purpose in her life, be more willing to wait for God to move, and learn to communicate more naturally with him all day long. Remember to pray today for your friend.

PRAYER FOCUS

"Father, reveal more of yourself to my friend this week as she prays and reads your Word."

FRIEND FOCUS

"God definitely dwells in the hearts of twosomes! When my prayer buddy prays for me, the windows of heaven open, blessing us both!"

—EDNA ELLISON

YOUR FOCUS

1 _____

2 _____

3 _____

For Remembrance

SCRIPTURE FOCUS

"It is right for me to feel this way about all of you, since I have you in my heart; for whether I am in chains or defending and confirming the gospel, all of you share in God's grace with me."

—PHIL. 1:7

I traveled with over 200 friends this last weekend more than halfway across the country and back. They weren't on the plane, but they were with me in prayer. I thought of their prayers when the plane wove its way through storms, when my energy levels dipped, and when the Spirit prompted me to completely rewrite my presentation the night before the event.

The morning of the Sunday prayerwalk kickoff, I got out of the shower and suddenly realized I had no comb or hairbrush. I had no car, the nearest store was a good half-mile away, and I didn't have time to get there and back. When I found out that the hotel desk clerk didn't have anything either, I jokingly asked, "Do you have a fork?" Even that silly incident was an answer to prayer: I had wanted to find a joke about myself that would let my audience know I'm an ordinary woman. So, later I told them: "I speak to you today with fork-ed hair!"

When we pray for each other, it's as though we become a part of each other's hearts. Our thoughts are like-minded and attuned to one another. We share in his grace as we remember to pray.

PRAYER FOCUS

"Lord, may many remember to pray for my friend this week—in thought, in prayer, in heart."

FRIEND FOCUS

"I know, no matter how large or small my request, my prayer partner takes it immediately to the Lord."

—BETTY SOUTHARD

YOUR FOCUS

1 _____

2 _____

3 _____

WEEK
28

For Courage

SCRIPTURE FOCUS

"Pray also for me, that whenever I open my mouth, words may be given me so that I will fearlessly make known the mystery of the gospel, for which I am an ambassador in chains. Pray that I may declare it fearlessly, as I should."

—EPH. 6:19, 20

We might fear heights or dog bites or car accidents. Personally, my greatest fear was encountering a skunk while I prayerwalked in the mornings. I say *was,* because a week ago I got sprayed and found out that it was not that big of a deal. My clothes took the brunt of it, and the smell washed away. The unknown can raise many fears—perhaps that's why we shy away from sharing our faith. The "what-ifs" permeate our thinking: *What if she thinks I'm pushy? What if she thinks I'm dumb? What if she doesn't like me anymore?* Now that I've been sprayed by a skunk and survived to talk about it, I've decided that talking about my faith isn't that scary after all!

We can support our prayer partner by praying that she has the courage to live out her faith in boldness—speaking to those in her life who are searching for purpose, for love, and for forgiveness. We can also pray that she will naturally give expression to her faith as she lives out her day—talking to and of God even when she is hurrying about her daily tasks. Another idea is to ask her for a list of those for whom she's praying to come into a relationship with God. I keep sticky notes plastered around my computer as visual reminders to pray for those I love. You have a great spot below to write down requests. Give her a call today and tell her you're praying!

PRAYER FOCUS

"Father, give my friend courage to share her faith fearlessly with those she loves."

FRIEND FOCUS

"Sometimes we need a prayer partner to take on the yoke that has us weighed down, even if it's just for a few moments. It's a gift we can give our women friends, a gift that comes with knowing Christ as the Lord of our lives."

—JANICE ELSHEIMER

YOUR FOCUS

1 _____

2 _____

3 _____

For Enemies

SCRIPTURE FOCUS

"Jesus said, 'You have heard that it was said, "Love your neighbor and hate your enemy." But I tell you: Love your enemies and pray for those who persecute you, that you may be sons of your Father in heaven.'"

—MATT. 5:43, 44

The first year I taught elementary school, I also was pregnant with our fourth child, Bethany. The first couple of months were especially rough because of morning sickness, and sometimes I had to apologize to my fourth and fifth graders for needing a breath of fresh air for a moment or two. While I was doing the best I could at my job, one mother of an underachieving girl complained that I was a bad teacher and that I used my pregnancy as an excuse to hide this "fact."

Ouch! After some tears and commiseration with teaching peers, one wise friend said that even when criticism she received was unjust, she had learned to turn it around and use it to make her a better teacher. From that experience, I learned to communicate more regularly with my students and their parents.

When our prayer partners are under fire—unjustly or otherwise—we can pray that the situation be turned around so that the experience makes them more Christ-like, that the relationship can be restored, and that through the entire process, God is glorified. That way, even if the enemy is behind the whole thing, the body of Christ is strengthened, and the kingdom of God grows.

PRAYER FOCUS

"Lord, teach my prayer partner to love even those who do not extend love to her."

FRIEND FOCUS

"It is such a blessing to have prayer partners who know, from personal experience, the specific challenges, temptations, and joys I encounter in my career."

—DEBRA RANEY

YOUR FOCUS

1 _____

2 _____

3 _____

For Discipline

SCRIPTURE FOCUS

"As for me, far be it from me that I should sin against the LORD by failing to pray for you."

—1 SAM. 12:23

I knew I was getting old when I started taping my to-do lists to my purse. One day, however, I realized I was even more ancient when I discovered I was forgetting to look at the taped-on list. That was when I decided that teenagers had the perfect solution: writing on their hands. I'm now famous—or infamous—for writing my lists on my left hand. I just have to make sure the job is done before I wash my hands!

Sometimes that task is prayer. One magazine photographer took a picture of my hand on which he had noticed names of friends for whom I pray: Hannah, Jared, and "smudge." No, that's not a name—I couldn't even read it!

I wouldn't consider it a sin if someone forgot to pray for me, but Samuel did. The people of Israel, who had again gone astray, had asked him to pray for them. Even though the Bible relates that they would ask him again to pray for them, Samuel answered them with exhortation and his promise to pray.

Sometimes we simply get busy and forget to pray. In those cases, I think God forgives us, and so we can forgive ourselves and each other, too. I have a sense that God prompts our prayer partner to pray when we have remembered her. As I'm sure she'd appreciate a reminder, pray that God helps her in her various spiritual disciplines.

PRAYER FOCUS

"Father, help my friend become more disciplined in prayer and in her life in general."

FRIEND FOCUS

"When I asked my prayer partner to pray for me as I tackled a project, she set aside time to come and brainstorm with me. Now that's a very valuable prayer partner!"

—JENNIE AFMAN DIMKOFF

YOUR FOCUS

1 _____

2 _____

3 _____

WEEK

31

For Fortitude

SCRIPTURE FOCUS

"May he strengthen your hearts so that you will be blameless and holy in the presence of our God and Father when our Lord Jesus comes with all his holy ones."

—1 THESS. 3:13

When my dad died several years ago, at first I felt as though the walls of my life were falling around me. Who would check my tires for me? Who would tell me when to get the oil changed? Who would call me "darling"? A few days after his death while I was watching my son play basketball at a final tournament game, I collapsed when my legs gave way from weariness.

After I put out word to a praying group of friends, however, I felt my strength return and even grow. At Dad's memorial service, I gave his eulogy without a single tear to the packed church and overflow crowd in the church hall—even urging others to leave this world a better place as he had. The prayers of my friends held me up during that difficult time.

When Paul prayed that the Thessalonians' hearts would be "strengthened," he used a classical Greek word that was generally used in the literal sense of putting a buttress on a building. That's exactly how I felt—as though folks were standing all around me, keeping me from collapsing— because of others' prayers for me. In case your prayer buddy needs your support this week, remember to ask the Lord to strengthen her in this way.

PRAYER FOCUS

"Father, give my friend emotional and spiritual strength this week."

FRIEND FOCUS

"My prayer partner opened up and showed me her heart and struggles, which allowed me to do the same. I discovered that she had struggled with the same obstacles in her extended family and therefore not only understood but knew exactly how to pray."

—T. SUZANNE ELLER

YOUR FOCUS

1 _____

2 _____

3 _____

For Favor

SCRIPTURE FOCUS

"But we ought always to thank God for you, brothers loved by the Lord, because from the beginning God chose you to be saved through the sanctifying work of the Spirit and through belief in the truth."

—2 THESS. 2:13

I was in a funk this afternoon, wearing the heaviness a mother wears when her child is choosing to make wrong decisions. He expressed his frustration with anger, specifically to hurt the ones he supposedly loves. Oh, prayer is hard work much of the time, especially when it's on behalf of children!

And then Carol called. She is our seventy-some-year-old church poet, famous for birthday and anniversary limericks and other delights. She didn't want to take a lot of my time, she said—she just wanted to thank me again for a little gift I'd given her months ago. She reminded me in her lighthearted way that God loves me and that she appreciated my friendship. "Could I pray for you?" she asked. "Is there some way that God could favor you with a special blessing?"

I told her that yes, there was. She prayed her lovely grandma-type prayer for my child, and I immediately felt peace that my children would restore their relationship.

Isn't it amazing how just a few kind words from a some-one can lighten your day? Your prayer friend could be in a similar funk today. Perhaps a simple reminder could help her remember that God loves her and allow her to let peace again reign in her heart.

PRAYER FOCUS

"God, favor my friend with gratitude from others this week."

FRIEND FOCUS

"I have two prayer buddies who hold me up regularly, whether I ask them to or not. I'm seldom surprised now when God wows me with his presence when I speak; he was invited to do just that."

—VIRELLE KIDDER

YOUR FOCUS

1 _____

2 _____

3 _____

For Holiness

SCRIPTURE FOCUS

"May God himself, the God of peace, sanctify you through and through. May your whole spirit, soul and body be kept blameless at the coming of our Lord Jesus Christ. The one who calls you is faithful and he will do it."

—1 THESS. 5:23, 24

It was not a good day. It was not a fun day. Somehow, though, my day of teaching seemed right—and I knew someone was praying for me somewhere.

After a series of challenging incidents, the most difficult moment came when a student cussed me out in my classroom quite publicly, thinking I had lost one of his assignments. That type of confrontation in the past would have put me on the defensive. This time, though, I sensed in my soul the words from Scripture: "In your anger do not sin" (Eph. 4:26).

I walked away, noted the incident on paper so I could deal with it later, and kept my mouth closed.

I also had the immediate knowledge that someone was praying for me and that, for some unknown reason, I needed on that particular day to be a good witness of my faith. It seemed as though my job—through all of the difficult circumstances—was a holy job that day, not because I was holy but because the faithful God at work in me was.

Within minutes after the student's outburst, he came to me with a paper extended. "I just found this, Mrs. McHenry," he said. "I turned it into the wrong box."

Prayer will help your buddy move toward holiness today.

PRAYER FOCUS

"Lord God, help my friend choose godly behavior today as she works."

FRIEND FOCUS

"There are many times that my prayer partner senses the spiritual tension in my life and begins praying long before I articulate the need. That sort of prayer partner is invaluable, as she can see the weather rolling in long before it starts to rain."

—ANITA RENFROE

YOUR FOCUS

1 _____

2 _____

3 _____

WEEK
34

For Teachability

SCRIPTURE FOCUS

"And we also thank God continually because, when you received the word of God, which you heard from us, you accepted it not as the word of men, but as it actually is, the word of God, which is at work in you who believe."

—1 THESS. 2:13

Earlier this year I remarked to a prayerwalking partner that I was impressed with the integrity of Balaam in the book of Numbers (see chapters 22 and 23). Immediately she responded, "Make sure you finish the whole book—he turns away from God later in his life." For some reason I'd never connected that the man who vowed to "do whatever the LORD says" (Num. 23:26) was the man who later turned the Israelites away from the Lord and to Baal worship (see Num. 31:16).

I am grateful for those mentors in my life who have pointed me to the Word, especially when I'm off-base or haven't seen the whole picture of a situation yet—either a biblical story or my own. I need those friends who will correct me and direct me along the paths of life.

Learning to accept teaching and correction from others is important to our growth as Christians. If we always have to be right, we get stuck in our own thinking and won't be open to God's direction in our lives. Learning from others and God's Word allows us to help others along their paths as well. One way to encourage a prayer partner is to send along a scripture verse, and perhaps that's just what your friend needs this week.

PRAYER FOCUS

"Father, help my friend remain open to your teaching—through your Word and through others around her."

FRIEND FOCUS

"How grateful I am that God doesn't intend for us to be Lone Rangers but gives us loyal prayer warriors to come alongside, lifting one another to the throne of grace to receive the mercy, grace, and help he has for us."

—CHERI FULLER

YOUR FOCUS

1 _____

2 _____

3 _____

For Decisions

SCRIPTURE FOCUS

"And this is my prayer: that your love may abound more and more in knowledge and depth of insight, so that you may be able to discern what is best and may be pure and blameless until the day of Christ, filled with the fruit of right-eousness that comes through Jesus Christ—to the glory and praise of God."

—PHIL. 1:9–11

During a season of writing when I became really busy, I knew I wouldn't be able to do my teaching job well if I didn't have some time off. However, I also didn't want to give up my job permanently. When I expressed my indecision to a teaching friend, Marla, she suggested that I take a sabbatical. Years ago, she had taken one in order to work on a master's degree. "I'll pray for you," she said, "and you'll know what to do." She was right. Just a month or so later, I applied for and received a half-year sabbatical to write a book about parenting and praying for teenagers. I know now the Lord had put my friend in just the right spot in my life to counsel me and pray for me as I decided what to do.

Making decisions isn't always easy, but we can find God's direction through several sources—the Bible, prayer, circumstances, and other people. Just because we're a prayer partner doesn't necessarily mean that we're also meant to be that friend's counselor. However, when you do pray for someone over a long time, God can speak to you on behalf of that person. In any case, praying is the best thing you can do to help your friend make the right decisions in her life.

PRAYER FOCUS

"Heavenly Father, give my friend discernment to make the right decisions this week."

FRIEND FOCUS

"Sometimes I would get stuck, and when an idea began lifting me out of the writing mire, I felt sure my partner in another state had prayed—even if she did not know my exact need at the moment."

—FRAN SANDIN

YOUR FOCUS

1 _____

2 _____

3 _____

For Hope

SCRIPTURE FOCUS

"I pray also that the eyes of your heart may be enlightened in order that you may know the hope to which he has called you, the riches of his glorious inheritance in the saints, and his incomparably great power for us who believe."

—EPH. 1:18, 19

Sometimes you know something's not right, simply because you've not heard from a friend in a long time. That was true for me with my friend Margaret. When I inquired via e-mail, she called. Life was tough. One child was hospitalized with an eating disorder. Another was creating havoc away at college. Her marriage was also about threadbare. "I'm not sure I'm going to make it through all of this," she said. "Let me pray for you," I said and asked God to be with her every step, giving her help and hope.

There are times when darkness falls so hard and so long that our friends lose sight of the light they have in Christ. Long-term illnesses, death, divorce, abuse, and other struggles can create heavy shadows. That's when, as prayer partners, we are called to remind our hurting sisters of the hope we have in Christ—that he is with us, that he has also walked that difficult road, and that he will carry us, never forsaking us. We can claim that hope for our friends, because he has chosen us as his daughters and has gifted us with power and promised us heaven.

Keep the hope fires burning for your prayer friend, so that light will overcome the darkness in her life.

PRAYER FOCUS

"Father, fill my friend with hope when she faces difficult times."

FRIEND FOCUS

"My long-time prayer partner carries my joys and my hurts to our heavenly Father. She daily lives Romans 12:15—'Rejoice with those who rejoice; mourn with those who mourn.'"

—SANDRA ALDRICH

YOUR FOCUS

1 _____

2 _____

3 _____

For Peace

SCRIPTURE FOCUS

"Do not be anxious about anything, but in everything, by prayer and petition, with thanksgiving, present your requests to God. And the peace of God, which transcends all understanding, will guard your hearts and your minds in Christ Jesus."

—PHIL. 4:6, 7

Two weekends ago, my family had a scare when the younger of Craig's and my two sons, Joshua, who was seventeen, had a medical emergency. When the EMTs rushed into the room, though, I knew everything would be okay. They were Ruth and her husband, Bruce; he drove the ambulance, and she attended to Josh.

I knew Ruth would do more than just take his vital signs as we traveled together in the ambulance. She's a dear Christian sister who has raised her children with the power of prayer. I knew she was joining me in petitioning our Father as we rode the forty-five minutes to the hospital. By the time we got there, Josh was cracking jokes with them and he was fine.

There's no way we can talk ourselves into the peace that passes understanding, because it doesn't make sense in human terms. The best thing we can do for our friends when they are troubled is to pray. When they're muddied with worry, we can help wash away the cares by praying with them and reminding them of our faithful Father who guards our hearts and minds in Jesus.

PRAYER FOCUS

"Lord, help my friend give her worries to you and fill her with your peace that passes understanding."

FRIEND FOCUS

"Even though we don't communicate frequently, it's such a comfort to know she's there, praying for me. A base of prayer is a podium of gold to stand on."

—DEB HAGGERTY

YOUR FOCUS

1 _____

2 _____

3 _____

For Communication

SCRIPTURE FOCUS

"I rejoice greatly in the Lord that at last you have renewed your concern for me. Indeed, you have been concerned, but you had no opportunity to show it."

—PHIL. 4:10

Yesterday morning God brought to mind my friend Stacy. I knew that the day before had been difficult: Her teenaged son had lashed out verbally, and she had barely made it through her workday. A couple days flew by, though, before I was able to give her a call to let her know I had been praying for her.

"You were?" she said. "I guess that's how I got through the last two days."

I have many of those kinds of days when I feel held up by the prayers of friends, even though I haven't expressed a need. It could be a day or a week or more later when I might run into someone and find out that I'd been on their praying mind.

My spirit feels lightened when a friend lets me know she's been thinking of and praying for me. Communication keeps us tied together. Certainly, it's wonderful if we can let our prayer buddies know that we're praying, but I think it's more important to lift up our sisters in Christ in prayer. There are countless stories about people waking in the middle of the night with the thought to pray for a family member or friend—just at a critical moment in the life of that person. Whenever your friend comes to mind this week, ask God to meet her deepest needs. You just never know when you're bringing heaven to earth for her.

PRAYER FOCUS

"Father, may many pray for my friend and let her know she's loved."

FRIEND FOCUS

"My prayer buddy and I have become dear friends and powerful and consistent prayer warriors over the past several years, standing in the gap for one another; we thank God for our prayer partnership and for one another."

—KAREN O'CONNOR

YOUR FOCUS

1 _____

2 _____

3 _____

For Troubles

SCRIPTURE FOCUS

"Is any one of you in trouble? He should pray. Is anyone happy? Let him sing songs of praise. Is any one of you sick? He should call the elders of the church to pray over him and anoint him with oil in the name of the Lord."

—JAMES 5:13

As I began to write tonight, I learned that my friend Carmen was suddenly and seriously ill at a women's conference. Her pain was excruciating; even so, she managed to speak and fulfill her commitment. A group of writer friends prayed for her until she flew home, until she got doctor's care, and until the pain had subsided—without the surgery that had been recommended while she was out of town.

As we mature in the faith, we learn that the challenging seasons of life become seasons of prayer. When we join together in prayer—even though miles and states separate us—we demonstrate to the world that we trust our faithful God. We teach those around us what it means to live out a life of faith. I believe the crises of life are like an open classroom: They show how Christians are different than those who do not believe. We care. We get involved. We invest in those we love.

When troubles hit, friends do not scatter; they gather in prayer, even when "gathering" may mean across miles and states and even oceans. When your prayer buddy faces difficulties, hit your knees in her behalf. Demonstrate to the world that our God is trustworthy in times of trouble.

PRAYER FOCUS

"Lord, lift the burden of my friend's troubles this week."

FRIEND FOCUS

"Though I have never met my prayer buddy in person, I know she will pray when I send an emergency e-mail request. It is a blessing to see her name when I open my e-mail, knowing she is standing—or kneeling—with me in prayer."

—LOUISE TUCKER JONES

YOUR FOCUS

1 _____

2 _____

3 _____

WEEK
40

For Maturity

SCRIPTURE FOCUS

"Epaphras, who is one of you and a servant of Christ Jesus,
sends greetings. He is always wrestling in prayer for you, that
you may stand firm in all the will of God, mature and fully
assured."

—COL. 4:12

I have Adelia's name posted on my desk. Because she prayed
to receive Christ with me this spring, I am wrestling in
prayer for her. An unemployed, single mom of two boys, she
returned home after the weekend retreat to many stresses. I
knew the enemy would not be happy with her new commitment, and so I remember her often before the Lord.

How can we wrestle in prayer for new believers so that
they can become mature and assured of their salvation? I pray
that they will believe the truth and not the lies that the
enemy may suggest. I told Adelia that when she doubted her

decision, that she should claim the date she prayed, remember her commitment, and thank Jesus for promising to never leave her or forsake her. I pray that she's reading her Bible, praying, and getting encouragement through regular fellowship with other believers. I also ask the Father to bind the enemy from interfering with her new faithful decisions.

Knowing that someone is praying can be a big encouragement to anyone—whether young or more mature in the faith. Join with your buddy this week for new believers she knows—and pray for their and her growth in the Lord.

PRAYER FOCUS

"Father, help my friend grow in her faith by leaps and bounds."

FRIEND FOCUS

"In my mid-twenties I partnered with a woman who was old enough to be my grandmother. She was a dear friend who helped me as a young woman."

—DEBRA WHITE SMITH

YOUR FOCUS

1 _____

2 _____

3 _____

For Compassion

SCRIPTURE FOCUS

"In their prayers for you their hearts will go out to you, because of the surpassing grace God has given you."

—2 COR. 9:14

When I am in need, I've learned to call upon trusted friends for prayer in my behalf. This has not come easily. I tend to think that I can take care of things myself— even prayer things. But as I've become more a part of others' prayer lives, I have developed wonderful friendships and have considered it a privilege to be asked to intercede. In turn, then, I've become more willing to let others help me in prayer, too.

In *The Way of a Pilgrim*, one of the pilgrim's mentors tells him that there are three kinds of prayers: verbal prayers, head prayers, and prayers of the heart. These aren't really explained, but I think that they're prayers we recite, prayers we discipline ourselves to pray, and prayers that grip our hearts—the kind that ache. When my friends are hurting, my heart aches, and I sense that God honors those prayers.

I don't know why, but when people are suffering, there are always those who only offer platitudes. Instead, genuine compassion, as expressed through prayer and kindness, gets us through those hurting times. One of the best gifts my family received was two large buckets of Kentucky Fried Chicken. Another was: "I've been praying for you all day long." Bearing our friends' burdens in prayer is a gift as good as two buckets of fried chicken! Let your heart ache as you pray this week for your buddy.

PRAYER FOCUS

"Father, let many touch my friend with compassion this week."

FRIEND FOCUS

"I can go to my praying sisters anytime, and they will totally understand my requests and intercede on my behalf. Everyone should have praying friends like this!"
—LUCINDA SECREST MCDOWELL

YOUR FOCUS

1 _____

2 _____

3 _____

For Forgiveness

SCRIPTURE FOCUS

"Jesus said, 'You have heard that it was said, "Love your neighbor and hate your enemy.'" But I tell you: Love your enemies and pray for those who persecute you, that you may be sons of your Father in heaven.'"

—MATT. 5:43–45

I often hear the conversations of my high-school students. Sometimes they're in the heat of anger about what "so-and-so" has done to them. Often, without pointing out anyone in particular, I'll say something like, "When someone makes you angry, who has the power in that situation?"

It always makes them pause and ponder for a few moments, but invariably they'll answer, "The other person."

Then I'll say, "And if you forgive that person, who has the power?"

They're quicker with this response: "I do!"

It's hard for anyone to forgive an enemy or someone who has caused hurt, but Christ has given us the power to do that through his Spirit, whose fruit includes love. One way I believe he grows this fruit in our lives is through the work of prayer. When I've prayed for those who have hurt me, somehow love and restoration are the eventual results of my prayers. Perhaps your friend needs to know forgiveness and restoration of broken relationships in her—or her family's—life. Pray that Christ will receive praise as the kingdom is mended.

PRAYER FOCUS

"Lord, let forgiveness reign over hurt and anger in my friend's heart."

FRIEND FOCUS

"Whether I am weeping or dancing before his throne, one of the great privileges of membership in the family of God is that he sends human partners to join me."
—REBEKAH MONTGOMERY

YOUR FOCUS

1 _____

2 _____

3 _____

43

For Wholeness

SCRIPTURE FOCUS

"May God himself, the God of peace, sanctify you through and through. May your whole spirit, soul and body be kept blameless at the coming of our Lord Jesus Christ. The one who calls you is faithful and he will do it."

—1 THESS. 5:23, 24

This summer at the book convention, I should have been excited about the release of my book that offers prayer strategies for parents of teens. Instead, I was on the verge of tears. My older son had called me the previous weekend; he was drunk, depressed, lonely—and emotionally on the edge. We talked for four and a half hours until 1:30 in the morning, and I prayed for another hour until the Lord gave me assurance that my son would still be living when the sun came up.

I shared my concerns with a few trusted friends—one of whom stopped me in the middle of the convention floor that week. "How old is your son?" she asked.

He'd be twenty-four in five months, I told her.

"Don't you remember what you wrote in your book?"

She reminded me that my research had found that 85 percent of prodigal children return to their Christian faith by the age of twenty-four . . . and then she prayed for my son: "You are faithful, Lord, and you will do it!"

When we're a little shattered by life's circumstances, our friends and their prayers can be the glue that puts us back together. Pray for wholeness for your friend this week.

PRAYER FOCUS

"Father, sanctify my friend—making her pure and whole."

FRIEND FOCUS

"The most powerful support of my prayer partner is that she remembers what God has promised, even when my heart is too full of despair to remember. She launches my faith to believe again."

—CRIS BOLLEY

YOUR FOCUS

1 _____

2 _____

3 _____

For Boldness

SCRIPTURE FOCUS

"I thank my God through Jesus Christ for all of you, because your faith is being reported all over the world."

—ROM. 1:8

In the same week, one prayer friend, Linda, was speaking to women of U.S. servicemen in Germany of the hope we have in Christ, while another friend, Carol, was extending the same message in China. As professional speakers, they annually speak to thousands about their faith on television and radio, as well as in person. Both of them have written in this book about how much they value the prayers of their friends. They truly are sharing their faith all over the world.

Our words may not be traveling the globe, but God can use our words of boldness when we talk to coworkers, neighbors, family members, friends, and even perfect strangers. We can unwrap the perfect present when we tell others of God's gracious gift of his son, Jesus, who gave his life so that we might live. My friend Linda did just that for me years ago when we were in college—absolutely the best gift anyone has ever given me. She took me to a movie produced by the Billy Graham Evangelistic Association called *For Pete's Sake*. In a small movie theater in a California university town, I not only made my personal commitment to Christ but also deepened my relationship with my dear friend, who has prayed for me through many struggles over the years, as I have for her. Pray that your friend takes bold steps to convey her faith this week.

PRAYER FOCUS

"Lord, help my prayer buddy love others in bold ways this week as she lives out her faith."

FRIEND FOCUS

"While I only see my prayer partner once a year, I can intercede for her every day. What a joy it is to know that someone with like passion and purpose is praying for me to impact the world for Christ."

—SHARON JAYNES

YOUR FOCUS

1 _____

2 _____

3 _____

For Enrichment

SCRIPTURE FOCUS

"I always thank God for you because of his grace given you in Christ Jesus. For in him you have been enriched in every way—in all your speaking and in all your knowledge— because our testimony about Christ was confirmed in you."

—1 COR. 1:4, 5

I am so thankful for my friends who pray for me. Not only do they pray for me, but they encourage me when I'm in creative and emotional slumps. When my editor asked me to take another year to work on a book project, my encouragers entered the picture. Their calls and e-mails helped me find my way past typical insecurities to know the truth. The truth was not the "you're-a-terrible-writer" noise I was hearing in my head, but instead what my friends were saying: "Wow! Your editor really believes in you!"

My friend Judy cemented this in a wonderfully visual way. She had six perfect red and yellow variegated roses delivered to my classroom at the high school where I teach. Not only did the flowers remind me that my friend loved me, but my students did as well when they said, "Wow, Mrs. McHenry. Someone thinks you're special!" I kept the roses until they dried to a crunch to remind me that God would help me craft each word as he had crafted those roses. With him, and with a little help from my friends, I would rewrite the book.

After you thank God today for how he has enriched your life through your prayer partner, ask him to encourage your friend in especially memorable ways.

PRAYER FOCUS

"Father, enrich my friend's life this week with your beautifully graceful gifts."

FRIEND FOCUS

"I value my friends who stand in the gap for me, for they are not just prayer partners—they are partners in ministry."

—JILL SAVAGE

YOUR FOCUS

1 _____

2 _____

3 _____

For Deliverance

SCRIPTURE FOCUS

"Pray that we may be delivered from wicked and evil men, for not everyone has faith."

—2 THESS. 3:2

Sometimes I feel as though I live in a protected nutshell here in my small mountain town in the northern Sierra Nevada. I have a ninety-second commute to work at school. I wave to everyone as I drive down Main Street, because I know them all. I walk without worry in the dark, early morning, because the most worrisome creatures are usually only raccoons or skunks.

But when I leave my shell to speak, I put my life into the hands of others as I travel. My prayer partners, a group of twenty-five men and women who pray for my writing and speaking, pray me through those goings and comings, and I step out without fear. Their prayers help me trust that God will protect me from the agents of the enemy, who would rather see me fail . . . or worse.

No matter if we travel for business or pleasure, we need protection from the crazies of this world who would do us harm. Additionally, with a single misjudgment, a serious car accident can change the lives of those involved forever. One of my friends says that many prayers can form a picket fence of protection around God's people. Plant those prayer pickets around your friend this week, so that she is guarded from all forms of harm.

PRAYER FOCUS

"Father, keep my friend from danger as she travels and goes about her daily tasks."

FRIEND FOCUS

"It is a relief to know my steps are surrounded by a hedge of prayer. This makes all the difference to my personal life and to the kingdom."

—LINDA EVANS SHEPHERD

YOUR FOCUS

1 _____

2 _____

3 _____

For Trust

SCRIPTURE FOCUS

" 'I cannot do it,' Joseph replied to Pharaoh, 'but God will give Pharaoh the answer he desires.' "

—GEN. 41:16

As the leader of a Moms in Touch group, I meet weekly in my high-school classroom with moms of teenagers for the purpose of prayer. Often they come heavily burdened with the baggage their teens have dumped on them—anything from substance abuse to indifference to the faith. As the teacher of these kids and a friend to these praying friends, I am tempted to solve their problems and take the pain away with specific how-to answers. I've had a lot of experience working with teens and may feel I know what I would do as a parent. The best thing I can do, however, is to pray—right then and daily thereafter.

As I conduct interviews about my book *Prayer Changes Teens: How to Parent from Your Knees,* I often talk with parents about their kids' problems. Sometimes the best advice I can give is, "I don't know all the answers, but I know where to go—to God." If your prayer buddy feels as though life is crashing around her right now, she probably doesn't need advice, Bible verses, scenarios, or stories. The best response is, "Let me pray for you right now." In the next day or so, get in touch with her and ask, "How can I pray for you, friend?" She will appreciate that you know where to go for her answers.

PRAYER FOCUS

"Lord, lead my friend to you for all of her answers this week."

FRIEND FOCUS

"My friend prayed for me that the Lord would ease the burden I felt over things that *must* be done in too little time. What a pleasure to share any trouble and know someone cares enough to pray with you."

—GAYLE ROPER

YOUR FOCUS

1 _____

2 _____

3 _____

For Devotion

SCRIPTURE FOCUS

"Be joyful in hope, patient in affliction, faithful in prayer."

—ROM. 12:12

How's my red-headed boy?" Sue would always ask within minutes of our meeting on the street or chatting on the phone. Sue had taught my son Justin, now twenty-four, when he was in Sunday school and seemingly had carved the names of her students on her heart.

She knew that Justin was at the top of my prayer list. When he started college, he "majored" in surfing for a couple years before he settled into academics. When Sue unexpectedly died a few months ago, Justin was still navigating the various identity channels, looking everywhere for the meaning of life . . . except into the eyes of the Savior, who had walked on water and calmed the seas.

I spoke of Sue's faithfulness in prayer for my son at her memorial service. I wish I'd been able to tell her that Justin had recommitted his life before she left hers here on earth. However, I sense that her faithful hours in prayer for my son will not be in vain, and I look forward to seeing her joy-filled face again someday and telling her, "Your prayers were answered, dear friend."

Your prayer buddy will appreciate your prayers for those long-term needs. Let her know this week that you are interceding in her behalf. She will be encouraged by your faithfulness.

PRAYER FOCUS

"Father, I pray that my friend is devoted in her study and prayer."

FRIEND FOCUS

"My most memorable prayer partner was an eighty-nine-year-old woman in our church who talked to me and talked to Jesus about me, all at the same time in a sort of three-way conversation."

—NANCIE CARMICHAEL

YOUR FOCUS

1 _____

2 _____

3 _____

For Action

SCRIPTURE FOCUS

"I pray that you may be active in sharing your faith, so that you will have a full understanding of every good thing we have in Christ."

—PHILEM. 6

I ran into a former student the other day. When Nicole saw me, she rushed over and hugged me, saying, "Mrs. McHenry, you were right! You were right!"

I laughed and said, "Yes, probably—but about what?"

"About boys!" she answered. "It's not about boys!"

When she was in high school, I continually reminded her that her future wouldn't be centered on the boys who then were all consuming for her and her friends. I recognized her creative gifts and compassion for others. Several years later, she recommitted her life to Christ, and now she and her dear Christian husband are leading a church youth group.

"You just keep doing what you do!" she said that day.

When we parted, we agreed we'd both pray for each other as we now minister in our different ways to teenagers in our valley.

Our greatest witness sometimes isn't an overt message—especially when we're not in a position to share our Christian faith. We can actively encourage others to pursue the God-given gifts we see in them, so that they are led toward God. Your prayer buddy will appreciate prayers for her this week—that she might live out her faith in practical ways.

PRAYER FOCUS

"Father, may my friend's witness be evident this week—even without a word."

FRIEND FOCUS

"These partnerships have afforded me the blessing of watching God work in another person's life. Double the fun! What a privilege to have a front-row seat for God's work in their lives."

—JENNIFER KENNEDY DEAN

YOUR FOCUS

1 _____

2 _____

3 _____

WEEK
50

For Children

SCRIPTURE FOCUS

"I have no greater joy than to hear that my children are walking in the truth."

—3 JOHN 4

I have a few friends in prayer whose sons, like mine, are choosing to take the circuitous, rocky path of life, rather than the one led by our faithful Guide. Whenever we chat on the phone or e-mail, inevitably the discussion will start or end up with "How's . . . ?" Whether or not my son is doing well at that point, the inquiry always encourages me, because I know that he's on the heart of my friend, who's helping me bear the prayer burden.

Our circle of children may even be larger than those given to us by birth. One of my "kids" just called a few minutes ago. Another Justin, he said, "Did I leave my wallet in your car?" Sure enough he did, in his golf bag. You see, I'm coaching the golf team this year, and now I've added another half dozen guys to my prayer-kid lineup. He knows that he can drop into my house any time of the day or night if he needs a place to hang out or sleep or eat. So, I count on my prayer friends to include those extra "kids" in their prayers as they remember my family and me.

As you pray for your buddy this week, remember her children as well—her own and those she influences. Someday you'll share in her joy as she relates to you that they are, indeed, walking in the truth.

PRAYER FOCUS

"Father, may my friend's children always walk in your truth."

FRIEND FOCUS

"My prayer partner and I both share a big heart for our daughters, so that's a bond that really holds us together in prayer."

—SUSAN WALES

YOUR FOCUS

1 _____

2 _____

3 _____

For Marriage

SCRIPTURE FOCUS

"Glorify the LORD with me; let us exalt his name together."

—PS. 34:3

After our small-town church split, my husband, Craig, stopped going. For several more years, I kept going, taking our kids to Sunday school and church. I even kept teaching an adult class. Each morning as worship would begin, I'd leave a vacant seat to my left in the back row, hoping that Craig would surprise me and slip in beside me. When minutes would tick off, I'd bite my lip, fighting back tears that'd inevitably fall anyway.

Many friends were with me in prayer over those years. In fact, some of them knew what it felt to be a Sunday widow, and I was praying for their husbands and them as well. Finally, four years later, Craig said, "Why don't we go to church together again?" It was painful leaving the church to which I'd belonged for more than twenty years—the church where our four children had publicly professed their faith and had been baptized. But as painful as it was, it was the right thing to do.

So, now my friends' prayers on my behalf have been answered. My kids, Craig, and I spend the Lord's Day together again in church. We also enjoy lunch out together and spend the afternoon doing something fun.

Pray this week that your prayer friend and her husband will spend their lifetime worshipping God together. If she is not married, pray that God meets her deepest needs for companionship with the Lord and with those who love him.

PRAYER FOCUS

"Father, bless my friend's marriage and may she and her husband glorify and worship you."

FRIEND FOCUS

"When our husbands were all in a professionally tough place, my prayer partner, another friend, and I got together weekly to pray for our husbands and marriages. We affectionately called ourselves the 'Praying Wives Club,' and our husbands really appreciated that we cared enough to partner in prayer on their behalf."

—MARITA LITTAUER

YOUR FOCUS

1 _____

2 _____

3 _____

For Friendship

SCRIPTURE FOCUS

"Thanks be to God for his indescribable gift!"

—2 COR. 9:15

My friend Hannah is God's indescribable gift to me. Whenever I call with one crisis or another, she says, "I'm coming down." Minutes later she's at my door ready to sit down, take my hands in hers, and pray. I always know I will be all right when Hannah prays. Life may still be a storm, but I will again be centered in God's peace and will weather whatever's ahead.

Today, then, when I heard that her mom would be leaving the hospital for hospice care at home, I started praying for her. "Are you feeling the love vibes?" I said into her cell phone's message recorder this evening.

The Swedish proverb says, "Friendship doubles our joy and divides our grief." Perhaps prayer for a friend does even more than that, because we can call upon the heavens to rejoice when we're rejoicing and we can ask our Lord to bear our pain and fill us instead with his peace. All I know is that when my friends, such as Hannah, pray with me, I am changed. I am reminded of God's great provision, his sovereignty, his love, and his purpose. My friendships of prayer are invaluable, because these wonderful people point me to the indescribable gift—God's son, Jesus Christ.

PRAYER FOCUS

"Thank you for my prayer partner, for our friendship, and for the indescribable gift of your son, Jesus Christ."

FRIEND FOCUS

"When my prayer buddy and I end our weekly prayer times together with tears running down our cheeks, we are not embarrassed, for we know we've touched each other's heart, as well as the heart of God."

—JEANNE ZORNES

YOUR FOCUS

1 _____

2 _____

3 _____